Walking the
LLANGOLLEN
CANAL

by
John N. Merrill

2006

The Canal Walk Series

THE JOHN MERRILL FOUNDATION

THE JOHN MERRILL FOUNDATION
32, HOLMESDALE,
WALTHAM CROSS, HERTFORDSHIRE,
ENGLAND. EN8 8QY

Fax – 01992-762776
email – marathonhiker@aol.com
www. walking_books.com

International Copyright © John N. Merrill . All rights reserved. No part of this publication may be reproduced or transmitted in any form or by any means electronic or mechanical including photocopy, recording or any information storage or retrieval system in any place, in any country without the prior written permission of The John Merrill Foundation.

The right of John N. Merrill to be identified as the author of this work has been asserted by him in accordance with the Copyright, Designs and Patents Act, 1988.

Typeset and designed by The John Merrill Foundation
Printed and handmade by John N. Merrill.

©Text - John N. Merrill, HonMUniv. 2005.
© Photographs, Maps & sketches - John N. Merrill, HonMUniv, 2005.

ISBN 1-874754-017-3
First published - July 1999. Reprinted & Revised December 2005.

British Library Cataloguing-in-Publication Data. A catalogue record of this book is available from the British Library.

Typeset in Hoefler Text, italic, and plain 11pt, 14pt and 18pt
Main titles in 18pt .**Stone Sans,** by J. Merrill in Adobe Pagemaker
on a Apple Macintosh.

Please note - *The maps in this guide are purely illustrative. You are encouraged to use the appropriate 1:25,000 O.S. Explorer map.*

John Merrill has walked all the routes in this book. Meticulous research has been undertaken to ensure that this publication is highly accurate at the time of going to press. The publishers, however, cannot be held responsible for alterations, errors, omissions, or for changes in details given. They would welcome information to help keep the book up to date.

Cover photograph by John Merrill
©The John Merrill Foundation 2005.

A little about John N. Merrill

Few people have walked the earth's crust more than John Merrill with more than 180,000 miles in the last 32 years - the average person walks 75,000 miles in a lifetime. Apart from walking too much causing bones in his feet to snap, like metal fatigue, he has never suffered from any back, hip or knee problems. Like other walkers he has suffered from many blisters, his record is 23 on both feet! He wears out at least three pairs of boots a year and his major walking has cost over £125,000. This includes 100 pairs of boots costing more than £11,800 and over £1,900 on socks - a pair of socks last three weeks and are not washed!

His marathon walks in Britain include - -

Hebridean Journey....... 1,003 miles. Northern Isles Journey......913 miles.
Irish Island Journey ....1,578 miles.   Parkland Journey.......2,043 miles.
Land's End to John o' Groats.....1,608 miles.
The East of England Heritage Route - 450miles.

and in 1978 he became the first person to walk the entire coastline of Britain - 6,824 miles in ten months.

In Europe he has walked across Austria - 712 miles - hiked the Tour of Mont Blanc, the Normandy coast, the Loire Valley (450 miles), a high level route across the Augverne(230 miles) and the River Seine (200 miles) in France, completed High Level Routes in the Dolomites and Italian Alps, and the GR20 route across Corsica in training! Climbed the Tatra Mountains ,the Transylvanian Alps in Romania, and in Germany walked in the Taunus, Rhine, the Black Forest (Clock Carriers Way) and King Ludwig Way (Bavaria). He has walked across Europe - 2,806 miles in 107 days - crossing seven countries, the Swiss and French Alps and the complete Pyrennean chain - the hardest and longest mountain walk in Europe, with more than 600,000 feet of ascent! In 1998 he walked 1,100 miles along the pilgrimage route from Le Puy (France) to Santiago (Spain) and onto Cape Finisterre; in 2002 walked 700 miles from Seville to Santiago de Compostela. In 2003 he walked 650 miles through the length of Portual via Fatima to Santiago de Compostela (Spian); 400 miles from Oslo to Trondheim, following St. Olav's Way, and all the trails on the Hong Kong Islands.

In America he used The Appalachian Trail - 2,200 miles - as a training walk, before walking from Mexico to Canada via the Pacific Crest Trail in record time - 118 days for 2,700 miles. Recently he walked most of the Continental Divide Trail and much of New Mexico; his second home. In 1999 he walked the Chesopeake & Ohio Canal National Historical Trail. In 2,000 he became the first thru hiker to walk 1,340 miles around Ohio, following the Buckeye Trail. In Canada he has walked the Rideau Trail - Kingston to Ottowa - 220 miles and The Bruce Trail - Tobermory to Niagara Falls - 460 miles.

In 1984 John set off from Virginia Beach on the Atlantic coast, and walked 4,226 miles without a rest day, across the width of America to Santa Cruz and San Francisco on the Pacific coast. This is one of the finest and most memorable walks, being in modern history, the longest, hardest crossing of the U.S.A. in the shortest time - under six months (178 days). The direct distance is 2,800 miles.

Between major walks John is out training in his own area - The Peak District National Park. He has walked all of our National Trails many times - The Cleveland Way thirteen times and The Pennine Way four times in a year! He has been trekking in the Himalayas five times. He created more than forty challenge walks which have been used to raise more than £700,000 for charity. From his own walks he has raised over £110,000. He is author of more than 260 walking guides which he prints and publishes himself, His book sales are in excess of 3 1/2 million, He has created many long distance walks including The Limey Way, The Peakland Way, Dark Peak Challenge walk, Rivers' Way, The Belvoir Witches Challenge Walk, The Forest of Bowland Challenge. the Dore to New Mills Challenge Walk , the Lincolnshire Wolds "Black Death" Challenge Walk and the Happy Hiker (White Peak) Challenge Walk and Jennifer's Challenge Walk. His new Pilgrim Walk Series includes the 36 mile, "Walsingham Way" - King's Lynn to Walsingham and St. Winefride's Way in Flintshire. He is currently writing a series of books about walks north of London. In January 2003, he was honoured for his walking and writing, recieving a Honorary degree, Master of the University, from Derby University. He lectures extensively about his walking.

CONTENTS

INTRODUCTION

I had been aware of the Llangollen Canal for many years, especially the Pontycysyllte Aqueduct, as you cross it walking the Offa's Dyke path. I had also on different occasions walked a section of the canal for various guidebooks, including my *"Long Circular Walks in Cheshire"* and my *"The Sweet Peak Challenge Walk."* But I had never walked it end to end! Then I had to chance to do it by boat and took the opportunity. I enjoyed it but felt I had lost contact with the "land" by not walking it, so I planned to do it again on foot. This was in 1996 but somehow other walks came in the way and the plan gathered dust on *"my walks to do shelf"*. Then in 1999, I walked the Chesapeake & Ohio Canal in America - one of their National Trails. Back in Britain I espied my Llangollen file and set off the following week! The plan was simple; start at Nantwich and follow a section of the Shropshire Union Canal to Hurleston Junction and the start of the Llangollen Canal. The first campsite close to the canal was at Grindley Brook, fifteen miles away so that would have to do for the first day. The next day of about 15 miles to Ellesmere and another campsite. A short day but Ellesmere is worth exploring. The final day to Llangollen and Horseshoe Falls would be the longest but with so many canal features to see it would prove to be a rewarding day.

The canal is a masterpiece of 18th century canal building and has no equal anywhere in the world. During July and August it is busy with boats, but in early June, with early summer still in the air, there were few boats and people and had the canal to myself. Apart from a couple of people walking their dogs I met not other walkers on the towpath or Offa's Dyke. The Nantwich Tourist Office suggested I could leave my car at Nantwich Marina and this I did, so I was immediately on the Shropshire Union Canal. Getting back I thought might be a problem but there was a frequent bus service requiring three changes. I had expected there to be a bus from Wrexham to Nantwich but the bus company jokingly said *"You have just missed it; the last one left THIRTY years ago!"*

By 10.30 a.m. I was walking along the Shropshire Union Canal, heading northwards to Hurleston Junction and the start of the Llangollen Canal, two miles away. Crossing the footbridge at the junction I walked past the flight of locks and began to following the towpath. The sun shone from a cloudless sky and for the three days I had cool but perfect walking weather. I soon came to my first lift bridge, a feature of the Llangollen Canal. Then onto Wrenbury and its mill and two inns. By late afternoon I approached the lock flight at Grindley Brook and called in the shop beside them to ask about the campsite. The map illustrated a site towards Whitchurch but the shop owner informed it was closed and a new one was opposite the lock! I walked across the lock gate to the house and was taken to camp warden who told me to pitch my tent beside a table and chairs beside the lock. What a perfect site! I sat in the sun watching the boats come through the locks. Later I walked down them to an inn for a meal.

The next morning I was walking before 8.0 a.m. and walked past the Whitchurch arm and walked into more remote countryside as I neared Whixall Moss and the Prees Branch, which forms part of my Sweet Pea Challenge Walk. I had had to make a detour as the towpath was closed. The section from Prees Branch past Whixall Moss to Ellesmere was a sheer delight with pine trees and numerous picnic tables placed by the Shropshire Union Canal Society. The scenery was rich countryside and more like "mountainous" than being on the plain. Nearing Ellesmere I passed the mere's, a feature of the area. Beside Blake Mere I had lunch but more than half my bread was eaten by the mallards and the swans with their cygnets. Walking into Ellesmere via its arm I walked through the town to the campsite, set in a peaceful dale.

The rest of the day was spent exploring the canal town and visiting the church, The Mere and heron observation point and castle. In the shops I stocked up with food before having the *"special Offer"* of a steak in the Ellesmere Hotel. I had decided to walk light-weight and carry no stove or cutlery. As I walked through the town the next day I stopped in a cafe for an early bird breakfast! .... I wasn't going to loose weight on this walk! Back on the towpath I soon had to leave it as it was closed and walked across the fields to rejoin the canal at the junction with the Montgomery Canal. The latter canal is being restored with locks being rebuilt and sometime in the future you will be able to go by boat along its length.

The scenery was now becoming more hilly as the Welsh hills came into view. First it was onto Chirk where there was a handy shop before the start of the climax to the walk and canal. Rounding a bend it was onto Chirk Aqueduct before walking through Chirk Tunnel. Then it was a little lull before the world famous Pontycysyllte Aqueduct. A delightful walk across with impressive views below and above; even the boaters didn't know where to look. At the end was the Trevor arm. Here I walked under the canal to pickup the final four miles of the canal to Llangollen. The canal hugs the valley side and is sometimes very narrow. Beside Llangollen the canal was busy with boats and here the canal end for the boaters.....but not for the walkers! There is two miles to go to Horse-shoe Falls where Thomas Telford created a semi-circular falls on the River Dee to feed the canal. It is a fitting end in the *"mountains"*. This solitary act was the canal's salvation for the canal acts as a water course and feeds the Hurleston Reservoir, 46 miles away, and was never closed. Boaters have to battle the current to Llangollen but helps them on their return trip!

Having reached the end it was two miles back to Llangollen. I thought of stopping after 26 miles of walking, but caught the bus to Wrexham. Here stepped immediately onto

6

one for Chester. Here I had to wait for the Hanley (Stoke on Trent) bus which goes via Nantwich. It passes the marina and three hours from Llangollen I was back at the start! It had been a wonderful three day walk through delightful scenery from the Cheshire Plains to the Welsh Hills. I hope the sun shines for you as you make your way along the King of canals.......*Happy walking! John N. Merrill.*

The Pontycysyllte Aqueduct.

HOW TO DO IT.

The following 1:50,000 Ordnance Survey Landranger maps cover the entire walk -

No. 118 - Stoke-on-Trent & Macclesfield
No. 117 - Chester & Wrexham & Ellesmere Port
No. 126 - Shrewsbury & surrounding area

I walked the route as a backpacking trip but you can do it in stages or by using the numerous accommodation places en route, as detailed later in the guide. There are campsites and accommodation at both Nantwich and Llangollen. It is walk not to be rushed and although I took three days it would make a perfect 4 day walk with a schedule of -

Day One - Nantwich to Whitchurch - 17miles
Day Two - Whitchurch to Ellesmere - 15 miles
Day Three - Ellesmere to Chirk- 12 miles
Day Four - Chirk to Horseshoe Falls and Llangollen- 10 miles

I left my car at Nantwich Canal Centre where they have a Visitors Parking Scheme - register in the Marina Shop - Tel. 01270 - 625122. The Nantwich Tourist Office can also help in suggesting where to leave your car. Nantwich is also well served with buses and trains with Crewe Station being closeby.

Being a canal walk there are many places to eat along the way, so food carrying is not necessary. There are also many shops - mostly signed from the canal - which also help reduce your load.

Getting back to Nantwich after the walk involves three buses - Llangollen to Wrexham; Wrexham to Chester; Chester to Nantwich (Hanley, Stoke on Trent bus). They all run at least hourly until mid evening.

<u>Tourist Offices -</u>

Nantwich - Church Walk, Nantwich, Cheshire. CW5 5RG. Tel. 01270 - 610983
Whitchurch - Tel. 01948 - 664577
Ellesmere - Meres Visitor Centre, Mereside, Ellesmere, Shropshire. SY12 0PA Tel. 01691 - 622981
Llangollen - Town Hall. Tel. 01978 - 860828
Wrexham - Lambpit Street - Tel. 01978 - 292015

ABOUT THE WALK
- some general comments.

Whilst every care is taken detailing and describing the walks in this book, it should be borne in mind that the countryside changes by the seasons and the work of man. I have described the walk to the best of my ability, detailing what I have found on the walk in the way of stiles and signs. Obviously with the passage of time stiles become broken or replaced by a ladder stile or even a small gate. Signs too have a habit of being broken or pushed over. All the route follow rights of way and only on rare occasions will you have to overcome obstacles in its path, such as a barbed wire fence or an electric fence. On rare occasions rights of way are rerouted and these ammendments are included in the next edition. Inns have a frustrating time of changing their name, then back to the original one!

The seasons bring occasional problems whilst out walking which should also be borne in mind. In the height of summer paths become overgrown and you may have to fight your way through in a few places. In low lying areas the fields are often full of crops, and although the pathline goes straight across it may be more practical to walk round the field edge to get to the next stile or gate. In summer the ground is generally dry but in autumn and winter, especially because of our climate, the surface can be decidedly wet and slippery; sometimes even gluttonous mud!

These comments are part of countryside walking which help to make your walk more interesting or briefly frustrating. Standing in a farmyard up to your ankles in mud might not be funny at the time but upon reflection was one of the highlights of the walk!

The mileage for each section is based on three calculations -

1. pedometer reading.
2. the route map measured on the map.
3. the time I took for the walk.

I believe the figure stated for each section to be very accurate but we all walk differently and not always in a straight line! The time allowed for each section is on the generous side and does not include pub stops etc. The figure is based on the fact that on average a person walks 2 1/2 miles an hours but less in hilly terrain. Allow 20 minutes to walk a mile; ten minutes for 1/2 mile and five minutes for 1/4 mile.

NANTWICH TO START OF LLANGOLLEN CANAL - 2 1/2 MILES

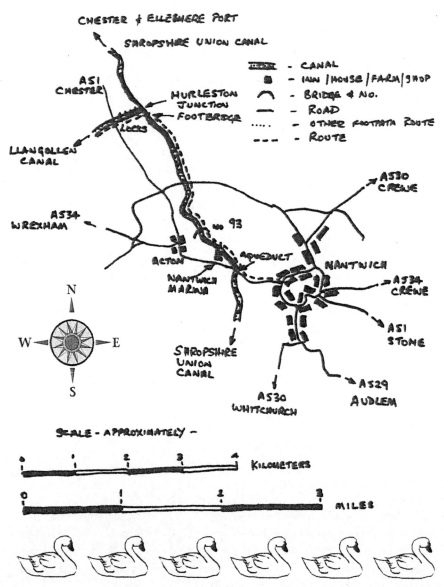

CHESTER & ELLESMERE PORT

SHROPSHIRE UNION CANAL

A51 CHESTER

HURLESTON JUNCTION
FOOTBRIDGE

LOCKS

LLANGOLLEN CANAL

	- CANAL
	- INN / HOUSE / FARM / SHOP
	- BRIDGE & No.
	- ROAD
.....	- OTHER FOOTPATH ROUTE
- - -	- ROUTE

A530 CREWE

A534 WREXHAM

No 93

ACTON

AQUEDUCT

NANTWICH MARINA

NANTWICH

A534 CREWE

A51 STONE

N
W E
S

SHROPSHIRE UNION CANAL

A530 WHITCHURCH

A529 AUDLEM

SCALE - APPROXIMATELY -

0 1 2 3 4 KILOMETERS

0 1 2 3 MILES

10

NANTWICH TO START OF LLANGOLLEN CANAL - 2 1/2 MILES

- allow 1 hour

 - Ordnance Survey 1:50,000 Landranger Series Sheet No.118 - Stoke-on-Trent & Macclesfield.

All facilities in Nantwich.

The Star Inn, Acton - three minutes from Bridge No. 93.

ABOUT THE SECTION - A short walk along the Shropshire Union Canal to Hurleston Junction; the start of the Llangollen Canal.

WALKING INSTRUCTIONS - From Nantwich follow the A534 road for Wrexham via the High Street and Welsh Row crossing the River Weaver. Soon afterwards approach the Shropshire Union Canal Aqueduct over the road and turn right and ascend to the canal. Turn right and keep the canal on your left. If starting from Nantwich Canal Centre, walk through the righthand side of marina along a track and cross a bridge over the canal and turn left. Keep the canal on your left and in 1/2 mile pass under Bridge No. 93 - The Star Inn at Acton is 3 minutes away! Half a mile later pass beneath the A51 road and on your left is Henhullbridge Moorings. In less than a mile reach a footbridge over the canal with the start of the Llangollen Canal on your left. Cross the Shropshire Union Canal to the Hurleston flight of locks at the start of the Llangollen Canal; keep the canal on your right.

NANTWICH - dates back to Roman times but has been burned down twice. Once by the Normans and the Great Fire of 1583 destroyed it. Nantwich was the only town in Cheshire to support the Parliamentarians during the Civil War. The Battle of Nantwich on January 25th 1644 is still re-enacted annually. The town has many timber-framed historic buildings and the 14th century church dedicated to St. Mary is known as the Cathedral of South Cheshire. Welsh Row is the oldest part of the town. If time permits Nantwich Museum is worth a visit and to see the spectacular Churche's Mansion on the A51 road.

THE SHROPSHIRE UNION CANAL - 66 1/2 miles long from Ellesmere Port to Autherley on the Staffordshire & Worcestershire Canal with 46 locks, was built by three separate companies between 1774 and 1835. In 1846 the Shropshire Union Railways and Canal Company was formed and became a major independent canal system that included the Llangollen and Montgomery Canals. Ellesmere Port was the busiest canal port until the 1940's and is now a major Boat Museum.

A BRIEF HISTORY OF THE LLANGOLLEN CANAL.

Originally it was planned to build a canal from Ellesmere (Port) on the River Mersey to Shrewsbury on the River Severn. An Act was passed in 1793 and the canal opened in 1805, but completely different from the initial plan and is basically what we see today. The canal engineers were firstly William Jessop and then Thomas Telford, whose masterpiece remains. The Shropshire Union Canal was originally known as the Chester Canal and goes to Ellesmere Port and this was opened in 1795. The section from Pontcysyllte to Llangollen and Horseshoe Falls (Llantisilio) was opened in 1808 as a navigable water feeder. This proved the saving of the canal for the water feeds the Hurleston Reservoir - 96 million gallons a week. The canal ceased being used by commercial traffic in the 1930's and in 1944 many canals were abandoned but the Llangollen was saved for its water supply. Today it is probably the most popular cruising canal in Britain and is certainly the most impressive and a magnificent engineering achievement that became a wonder of the world 200 years ago, and still inspire amazement . The key features are the Chirk Aqueduct and tunnel and the Pontcysyllte Aqueduct.

The canal is 46 miles long with 21 locks; the last ones being the New Marton Locks - the remaining 14 miles to Llangollen are lock free. Grindley Book has six locks - three ordinary locks followed by a three rise staircase lock. The bridges are numbered from 1 at Hurleston to No. 69 at the junction of the Montgomery Canal at Frankton Junction. Here the Llangollen Canal bridges start from No. 1 to No. 49 at Horseshoe Falls. The narrow boats are no more than 72 feet long by 6 ft 10" wide.

Further reading on the history of the canal and canals -
British Canals by Charles Hadfield. David & Charles 1979
The Ellesmere and Llangollen Canal by Edward Wilson. Philmore 1975

Further Information about the Llangollen Canal -
British Waterways,
Border Counties Waterway
Canal Offices,
Birch, Ellesmere,
Shropshire. SY12 9AA

Tel. 01691 - 622549

Chirk Aqueduct and tunnel.

HURLESTON TO WRENBURY - 6 MILES

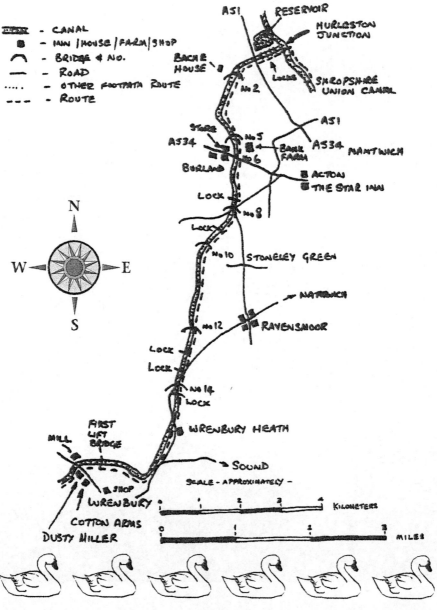

Legend:
- 〰〰 — CANAL
- ▪ — INN / HOUSE / FARM / SHOP
- ⌒ — BRIDGE & NO.
- — — ROAD
- ..... — OTHER FOOTPATH ROUTE
- - - - — ROUTE

A51
RESERVOIR
HURLESTON JUNCTION
BACHE HOUSE
No 2
LOCKS
SHROPSHIRE UNION CANAL
A51
STORE
A534
No 5
No 6
BACHE FARM
A534 NANTWICH
BURLAND
ACTON
THE STAR INN
LOCK
No 8
LOCK
No 10
STONELEY GREEN
NANTWICH
No 12
RAVENSMOOR
LOCK
LOCK
No 14
LOCK
WRENBURY HEATH
FIRST LIFT BRIDGE
MILL
SOUND
SCALE - APPROXIMATELY -
SHOP
WRENBURY
COTTON ARMS
DUSTY MILLER

N
W — E
S

KILOMETERS
0   1   2   3   4

MILES
0   1   2   3

HURLESTON TO WRENBURY - 6 MILES
- allow 2 hours

- Ordnance Survey 1:50,000 Landranger Series Sheet Nos.
- 118 - Stoke-on-Trent & Macclesfield.
- 117 - Chester & Wrexham

Stores - Burland and Wrenbury. Blackberry Farm (Home of some Rare Breeds) near Bridge No. 1, has a small shop and cafe.

- Wrenbury - The Dusty Miller and The Cotton Arms

ABOUT THE SECTION - First you pass the flight of four locks at Hurleston before levelling out along the canal past several more locks to the impressive mill at Wrenbury; you are in Cheshire the whole way. As you approach Wrenbury you come to your first lift bridge, a feature of the canal. There is a shop at Burland just over the canal after 1 1/ 2 miles and another at Wrenbury in the village.

WALKING INSTRUCTIONS - You keep the canal on your right for the whole length of this section to Wrenbury. First ascend beside the four Hurleston Locks to Bridge No. 1 (A51 road). Hurleston Reservoir is to your right which holds 8 million gallons of water. Then onto Bridge No. 2 with Bache House on the other side. More than a mile later gain Bridge No. 6 (A534 road) at Burland with Burland Stores on the otherside. Next pass the two Swanley Locks before reaching Bridge No. 10. More than 2 miles later pass the three Baddiley Locks before passing Wrenbury Heath on your left at Bridge No. 15. More than a mile later reach your first lift bridge and soon after Wrenbury Mill and electric lift bridge beside the Dusty Miller Inn.

WRENBURY - Small attractive village worth a visit. The shop is near the church dedicated to St. Margaret. The church has an interesting organ and box pews.

The Start of the Llangollen Canal at Hurleston Junction.

Lock House at the top of the Hurleston Flight.

The first Lift Bridge near Wrenbury.

Wrenbury Mill and electric Lift Bridge.

WRENBURY TO GRINDLEY BROOK
- 6 MILES ·

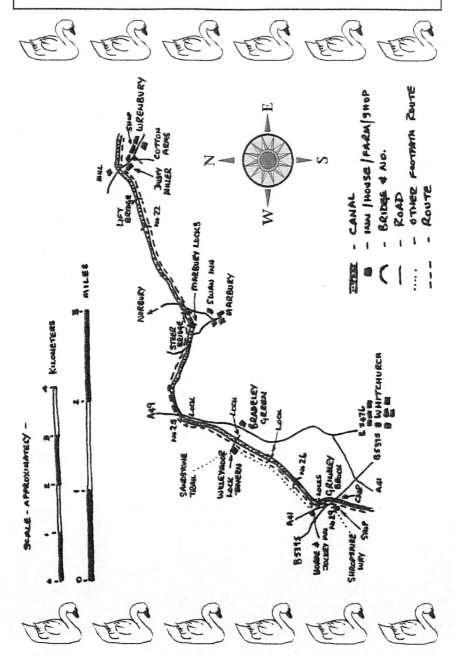

WRENBURY TO GRINDLEY BROOK
- 6 MILES
- allow 2 hours

 - Ordnance Survey 1:50.000 Landranger Series Sheet No. 117 - Chester & Wrexham

 - Stores - One in Wrenbury and two in Grindley Brook - beside the canal, on the right.

- Inns - Swan Inn, Marbury - 1/2 mile from Marbury Lock. Willeymoor Lock Tavern beside Willeymoor Lock. Horse & Jockey Inn in Grindley Brook.

ABOUT THE SECTION - A delightful walk and the section before Marbury Lock is particularly attractive with solitary pine trees. At Willey Moor Lock the canal towpath is also the final/ start of the Sandstone Trail - 32 miles to Beacon Hill, Fordsham. Here also the canal acts as the county boundary of Cheshire and Shropshire. Grindley Brook is also the start of a spur trail of the 139 mile Shropshire Way.

WALKING INSTRUCTIONS - Continue on the towpath from Wrenbury with the canal on your right. In two miles reach Marbury Lock and cross the canal and continue on the towpath with the canal on your left. Marbury lies 1/2 mile to the south and if time permits is well worth a visit to see the church and its impressive position above Big Mere. Continue to Steer Bridge No. 24 and less than a mile later Bridge 25 (A49) road and just after Quoisley Lock. Just over 1/2 mile later reach Willey Moor Lock, Tavern, and Sandstone Trail. !/4 mile later pass Povey's Lock and a mile later pass through a small tunnel before the three Grindley Brook Locks. To your right of them is a garage with shop and the Horse and Jockey Inn (meals). Continue on to the staircase lock (three locks) - the only staircase locks on the Llangollen Canal - with a shop beside the canal. On the other side is the campsite and road to Whitchurch. The place is worthy of a halt with so many amenities and boats to watch using the locks.

Willey Moor Lock and Tavern.

Grindley Brook Tunnel and view to first lock.

Grindley Brook Staircase Lock

Grindley Brook Campsite at the top of the Staircase Locks.

GRINDLEY BROOK TO PREES BRANCH - 7 MILES

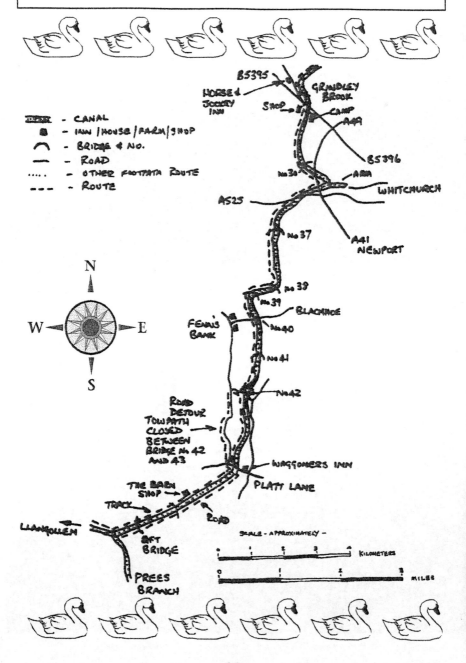

KEY

- ▦▦▦ – CANAL
- ◼ – INN / HOUSE / FARM / SHOP
- ◠ – BRIDGE & NO.
- — – ROAD
- ..... – OTHER FOOTPATH ROUTE
- - - - – ROUTE

N
W — E
S

B5395
HORSE & JOCKEY INN
SHOP
GRINDLEY BROOK
CAMP
A49
B5396
No.36
AREA
WHITCHURCH
A525
No.37
A41 NEWPORT
No.38
No.39
BLACKHOE
FENNS BANK
No.40
No.41
No.42
ROAD DETOUR TOWPATH CLOSED BETWEEN BRIDGE No.42 AND 43
WAGGONERS INN
PLATT LANE
THE BARN SHOP
TRACK
ROAD
LLANGOLLEN
LIFT BRIDGE
PREES BRANCH

SCALE - APPROXIMATELY -

0   1   2   3   4   KILOMETERS
0   1   2   3   MILES

GRINDLEY BROOK TO PREES BRANCH
- 7 MILES
- allow 2 1/2 hours.

- Ordnance Survey 1:50,000 Landranger Series Sheets Nos -
- 117 - Chester & Wrexham
- 126 - Shrewsbury & surrounding area

Stores - Whitchurch - 1/2 mile from end of the Whitchurch Arm.
- The Barn shop beside the canal 3/4 mile mile before Prees Branch.

- Several in Whitchurch - 1/2 mile from the end of the Whitworth Arm
- The Black Bear, Old Town Hall Vaults, The Greyhound Inn.
- Waggoners Inn, Platt Lane - 200 yards from Bridge No. 43.

ABOUT THE SECTION - A mile from Grindley Brook you reach the Whitchurch Arm - inns and shops are approximately 1/2 mile from here. Much of the section is delightful walking and I heard and saw curlew and skylarks; Canada Geese and their chicks were on the canal sides. The towpath between bridges 42 and 43 (Platt Lane) is closed and a road walk around negotiates the problem. Here you also do a part of my 25 mile Sweet Pea Challenge Walk from Wem. Approaching the Prees Branch you are entering the remotest and most beautiful section of the canal.

WALKING INSTRUCTIONS - From Grindley Brook continue on the righthand side of the canal and after passing under the A49 reach the swing bridge and Whitworth Arm in a mile. Continue on the towpath passing under the A49 again and then the A525 passing the Viking Afloat base on your left. Continue on the righthand side for more than a mile passing Bridges Nos 38, 39 and 40 with the road to Fenn's Bank. Little over 1/2 mile later reach the swing bridge No. 42 - beyond the towpath is unpassable. Turn right along the lane and in a short distance at the T junction turn left and 3/4 mile later left again to Bridge No. 43 . Just before it on your right is a track which you can follow soon bringing you back onto the towpath and past the Barn Shop. Alternatively you can cross the bridge - straight ahead at the end of the road on your left is the Waggoners Inn, Platt Lane - and turn right and walk along the lane beside the canal to the next bridge. Cross over to the cottage Mountain View - you can see the Welsh Hills from here! Turn left and are immediately back on the towpath; both routes join here. Little over 1/2 mile later pass a large car wrecking establishment to your right at the start of Whixall Moss and to your left the impressive canal house at the start of the Prees Branch.

The Whitchurch Arm.

Canal approaching a Lift Bridge.

Canada Geese and chicks on the canal side.

The Prees Branch.

PREES BRANCH - I have followed the line of the canal to near Quina Brook where it ended in 1806. The actual village of Prees is still 3 miles away. The branch is waterfilled for 1 1/2 miles and now acts as the entrance to Whixall Marina. The remainder of it is a Nature Reserve.

PREES BRANCH TO ELLESMERE
- 7 MILES

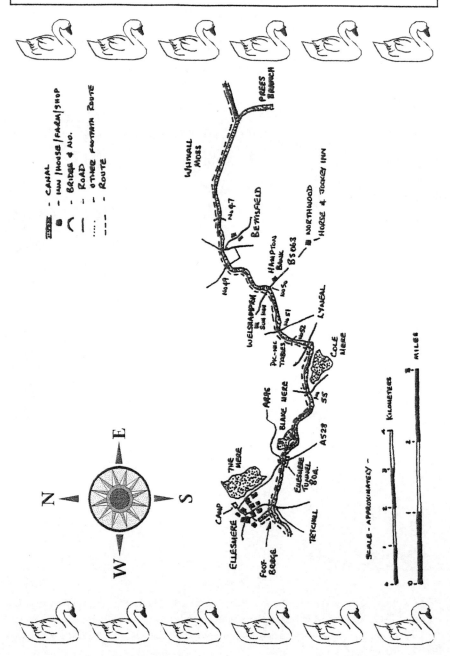

PREES BRANCH TO ELLESMERE
- 7 MILES
- allow 2 1/2 hours.

 - Ordnance Survey 1:50.000 Landranger Series Sheet No. 126 - Shrewsbury & surrounding are.

 Stores - Full amenities in Ellesmere.

 Inns - Horse & Jockey Inn, Northwood - 2000 yards south from Bridge No. 48. The Swan Inn, Welshhampton - 3/4 mile from Bridge No. 51. Numerous in Ellesmere including the Ellesmere Hotel and The Black Lion.

 - Accommodation - Hotels and B & B in Ellesmere. Camping at Talbot Caravan Park, Talbot Street, Ellesmere. Tel. 01948 - 875329.

ABOUT THE SECTION - Beautiful! A wide towpath on the right of the canal leads you through wonderful scenery of pine trees. The Shropshire Union Canal Society have placed several picnic tables along the route. I stopped by the one at Blake Mere where the ducks, swans and Canada Geese ate more of my food than I! After five miles you reach Colemere Country Park on your left before Blake Mere. After this you walk through the 80m long Ellesmere tunnel and 3/4 mile later reach the arm of the Ellesmere branch. There is much to see in Ellesmere and it makes a useful stocking up place ready for the climax to the walking the canal, tomorrow.

WALKING INSTRUCTIONS - Opposite the Prees Branch continue along the righthand side of the canal on a wide grassy towpath, with Whixall Moss on your right - they still cut peat here. It is a wonderful remote section for 1 1/2 miles to Bridge No. 48 at Bettisfield. Continue on the right and a mile later pass Hampton Bank. A further mile brings you past Lyneal Wharf at Bridge 53. Just after on your left is Cole Mere and Country Park. More than a mile later pass Blake Mere on your right. Soon afterwards walk through Ellesmere Tunnel - 80m (87 yards) long, under the A528 road. !/2 mile later cross the towpath bridge with Blackwater Meadow Marina on your right. Cross another bridge over the Ellesmere Arm (wharf) and turn right up it for Ellesmere. If wanting the campsite walk up Wharf Road to the Main Street and shops. Turn right and keep ahead soon walking along Cross Street to the A528 road. Turn right then left into Talbot Caravan Park.

ELLESMERE - A pretty Market Town with half timbered and mediaeval buildings and a Georgian Town Hall. The surrounding mere are remnants of the last ice-age 15,000 years ago. The retreating ice collected in these clay lined hollows. The Mere at Ellesmere is the largest - covers 116 acres and is 60 feet deep - and has a Visitor's Centre and Heron Observation Point - 19 pairs nested in 1999. The church dedicated to St. Mary is known as the "Cathedral of the Meres" and was built in 1225 by the Knights of St. John. Inside is a 15th century chapel and the churchyard has a gravestone to a man aged 104. Ellesmere was an important base being only 3 miles from Wales and the Norman's built a Motte and Bailey Castle here. A walk from Castlefields leads you to the site with views of The Mere.

Ellesmere - Canal Wharf.

The Llangollen Canal nearing Colemere Country Park.

Picnic bench with Blake Mere beyond

Ellesmere Tunnel.

Junction of the Ellesmere Arm.

Ellesmere Arm, looking towards the town.

Llangollen Canal near Tecthill.

ELLESMERE TO CHIRK BANK - 11 MILES

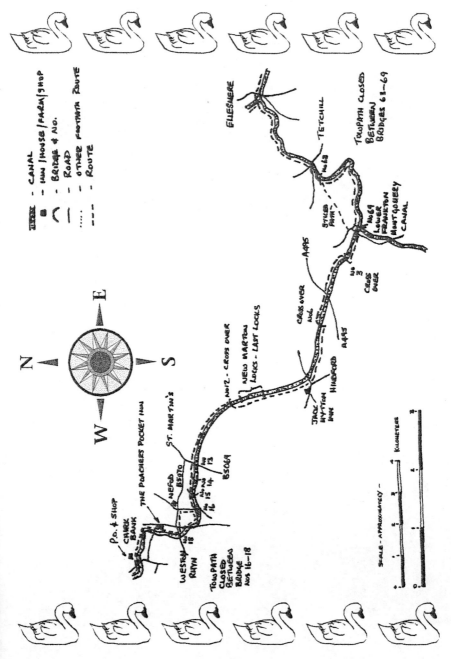

KEY

- ▬▬ = CANAL
- ■ = INN/HOUSE/FARM/SHOP
- ⌒ = BRIDGE & No.
- ····· = OTHER FOOTPATH ROUTE
- – – – = ROUTE

ELLESMERE

TETCHILL

TOWPATH CLOSED BETWEEN BRIDGES 63-69

STILES PATH

No 64 LOWER FRANKTON MONTGOMERY CANAL

A495

No 3 CROSS OVER

CROSS OVER A495

A495

No 2 - CROSS OVER

NEW MARTIN LOCKS - LAST LOCKS

HINDFORD

JACK MYTTON INN

ST. MARTIN'S

THE POACHERS POCKET INN

NEFOD

B5070

No 15 No 13

No 15 14

No 16 No 16

B5069

P.O. & SHOP

CHIRK BANK

WESTON RHYN

No 18

TOWPATH CLOSED BETWEEN BRIDGE Nos 16-18

SCALE - APPROXIMATELY -

KILOMETERS

ELLESMERE TO CHIRK BANK
- 11 MILES
- allow 4 hours.

 - Ordnance Survey Landranger Series Sheet No. 126 - Shrewsbury & surrounding area.

 Stores - Chirk Bank Post Office.

- The Narrow Boat Inn at Bridge No. 5. The Jack Mytton Inn, Hindford at Bridge No. 11. Plough Inn, Weston Rhyn - 8 minutes from canal Bridge No. 18. The Poachers Pocket beside canal at Chirk Bank. The Bridge Inn, Chirk Bank - the last inn in England - 75 yards from the canal.

ABOUT THE SECTION - Some beautiful walking with glimpses of the approaching Welsh Hills. You use several crossover bridges and walk with the canal on your right and left. The canal towpath is closed in two places; firstly from bridge No. 63 to the Montgomery Canal junction at Lower Frankton - a path over the fields misses this section with great views. Secondly from Bridge 16 to Rhosweil - you have to road walk around. The canal bridges start from 1 again after the junction with the Montgomery canal. Little over half way you pass the two New Marton Locks, the last on the canal. The final 14 miles are lock free to Horseshoe Falls. Chirk Bank has a combined shop and Post Office with an inn nearby. It is the lull before the storm...ahead is the masterpiece of canal engineering!

WALKING INSTRUCTIONS - Walk down the Ellesmere Arm and turn right keeping the canal on your left and walk along a good towpath for 1 1/2 miles to Bridge No. 63 - a track from Tetchill on your left. The next mile of the towpath is closed so leave the canal on your right - do not cross the bridge - and follow the track a few yards to a stile and pathsign on your right. Walk up the track/path passing a house on your left to a stile. The path bears slightly left now and is well defined at first to the next stile. Basically keep straight ahead for 1/2 mile; it is well stiled - you may have to walk around the fields - and aim for the righthand side of a white painted house - Brookside Cottage. As you do so you have views to the Welsh Hills. On the right of the cottage is a gate and track between the houses to a lane. Turn left and follow the lane to bridge No. 69 and the junction of the Montgomery Canal. Descend to the canal and follow the towpath on the righthand side of the canal to Bridge No 1. Crossover and walk along the lefthand side of the canal to Bridge No 3 and crossover. Continue on the righthand side of the canal to Bridge No 5 and the A495 road and on past the Narrow Boat Inn to the next bridge - No 6 and crossover. Now keep the canal on your left as you walk through Hindford and the Jack Mytton Inn on your left. 1/2 mile later pass the first lock of the New Marton Locks. After the second one you crossover at Bridge No 12 and keep the canal on your left all the way to Chirk and Trevor.

1 1/2 miles later at Bridge No. 16 the towpath is closed between here and Bridge No. 18. Turn right away from the canal and follow the lane to the road junction at Nefod, 1/4 mile away. Turn left along the B5070 road to the A5 roundabout - this is a short road walk but the busiest road and a stark contrast to the solitude of the canal. At the roundabout take the second road on your left to Weston Rhyn. 200 yards later you are back at the canal. Descend to your right and keep the canal on your left. There are no more "problems" between here and the end. 1/4 mile later pass The Poacher's Pocket Inn on your right and less than 1/2 mile later reach Chirk Bank and Post Office/Shop on your right.

THE MONTGOMERY CANAL - 35 miles long. Work began in 1968 to restore this canal and considerable work has been carried out with locks rebuilt. The canal was built in three separate sections and was completed in 1819. A breach in an aqueduct in 1936 resulted in traffic ceasing. Like many of the canals it was abandoned but in 1967 the Shropshire Union Canal Society did a study to see if it could be restored and thanks to their efforts a major restoration project is underway. Boats are now using the start of the canal and more of it as it becomes open.

Frankton Junction - Montgomery Canal going off to your right.

Crossover bridge - this ensured that the horse towing the boat always kept the rope attached to the boat.

The second of the New Marton Locks.

CHIRK BANK TO TREVOR - 4 MILES

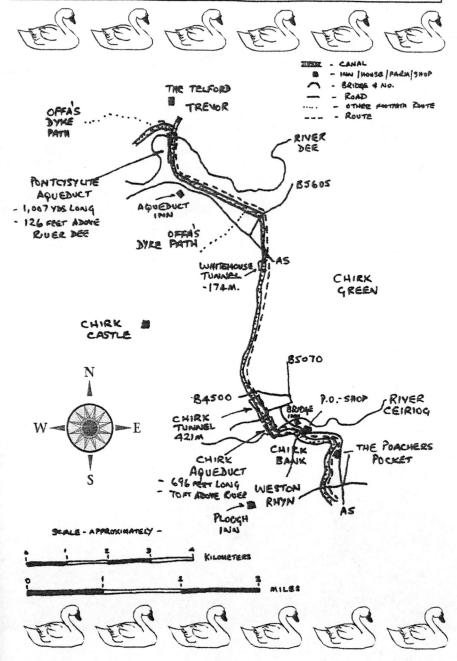

KEY:
- CANAL
- INN / HOUSE / FARM / SHOP
- BRIDGE & No.
- ROAD
- OTHER FOOTPATH ROUTE
- ROUTE

THE TELFORD
TREVOR

OFFA'S
DYKE
PATH

RIVER
DEE

B5605

PONTCYSYLTE
AQUEDUCT
- 1,007 YDS LONG
- 126 FEET ABOVE
RIVER DEE

AQUEDUCT
INN

OFFA'S
DYKE PATH

AS

WHITEHOUSE
TUNNEL
- 174 M.

CHIRK
GREEN

CHIRK
CASTLE

B5070

B4500

P.O.-SHOP

RIVER
CEIRIOG

CHIRK
TUNNEL
421M

BRIDGE
INN

THE POACHERS
POCKET

CHIRK
AQUEDUCT
- 696 FEET LONG
- 70 FT ABOVE RIVER

CHIRK
BANK

WESTON
RHYN

AS

PLOUGH
INN

N
W   E
S

SCALE - APPROXIMATELY -

0   1   2   3   4   KILOMETERS

0   1   2   3   MILES

36

CHIRK BANK TO TREVOR
- 4 MILES
- allow 2 hours.

- Ordnance Survey Landranger Series Sheets Nos -
- 126 - Shrewsbury & surrounding area.
- 117 - Chester & Wrexham

Stores - Trevor.

- The Aqueduct Inn; Britannia Inn; Froncysyllte. The Telford, Trevor.

ABOUT THE SECTION - Stunning! Almost immediately you walk across the Chirk Aqueduct, a foretaste of what is to become. Then you enter the longest tunnel - 421m before the two mile "lull" before the incomparable Pontycysyllte Aqueduct into Trevor. The last mile is also part of the 186 mile Offa's Dyke National Trail. This section should not be hurried but savoured for nowhere else in the world is there such a masterpiece of 18th century engineering and the setting of the Welsh Hills make it unforgettable.

WALKING INSTRUCTIONS - Continue beside the canal on your left on a tarmaced surface and soon pass a house on your right with some historic canal plaques on the walls. Immediately afterwards beginning crossing the Chirk Aqueduct. At the end is the 421 metre long Chirk Tunnel. There is a path over it as detailed on the Information boards, but I would strongly encourage you to walk through the tunnel in keeping with the spirit of the canal travel. There is a good towpath with hand rail. I did not use a torch but used the rail as my guide. After the tunnel the canal passes through an embankment with Chirk Castle to your left, although hidden. After emerging into the open you pass Chirk Marina before walking through the 174 metre long Whitehouse Tunnel - there is a path over this as well. A mile later Offa's Dyke Path joins the towpath as the canal contours round above the River Dee (Afon Dyfrdwy) to the Pontycysyllte Aqueduct. Take your time crossing to admire the view and drop! At the end gain Trevor.

CHIRK TUNNEL - 421 metres (459 yards) long.

CHIRK AQUEDUCT - Overshadowed by the railway bridge on the left. The stone channel is 70 feet above the ground and River Ceirog.

CHIRK CASTLE - A signed path leads to the 14th Century Castle cared for by the National Trust, a mile away.

WHITEHOUSE TUNNEL - 174 metres (191 yards) long.

Chirk Aqueduct and tunnel beyond.

PONTYCYSYLLTE AQUEDUCT - Engineering by Thomas Telford it is more than 1,000 feet long and 126 feet above the River Dee and has 19 arches. There is a towpath on the righthand side but just 2 " of metal on the left - quite exhilarating in a narrowboat! It took 10 years to build and was opened in 1805.

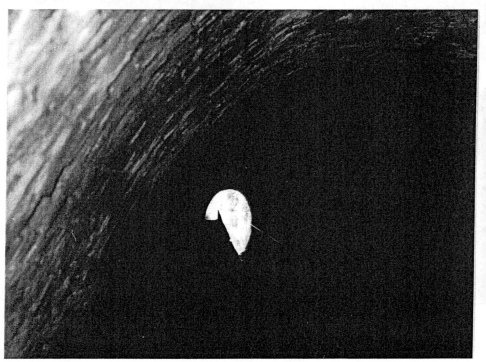

Chirk Tunnel inside and out.

TREVOR TO HORSESHOE FALLS & LLANGOLLEN - 8 MILES

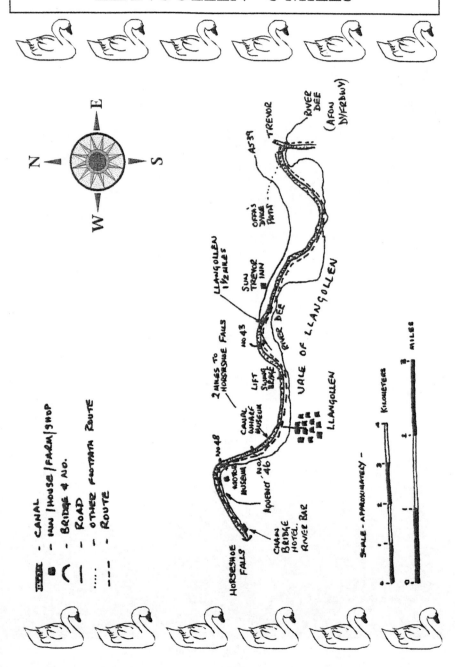

TREVOR TO HORSESHOE FALLS & LLANGOLLEN - 8 MILES
- allow 3 hours

- Ordnance Survey Landranger Series Sheet No. 117 - Chester & Wrexham.

Stores - Trevor and Llangollen.

- Sun Trevor - opposite the canal beside the A542 road, reached via a bridge. Chain Bridge Hotel & River Bar close to the end before Horseshoe Falls.

- Llangollon Canal Wharf and numerous in Llangollen.

ABOUT THE SECTION - Sadly the final section following the very narrow canal - in some places only one boat can pass - as it hugs the valley side to Llangollen. Here the boats stop but the walk and canal extend another 2 miles to Horseshoe Falls, making a very fitting end to the walk amidst the Welsh Hills. You have to retrace your steps back to the Canal Museum and descend into Llangollen for rest, accommodation, transport, food ..... and return, alas.

WALKING INSTRUCTIONS - Just after crossing the Pontcysylltye Aqueduct with its plaque to the builders, turn right and follow the Offa's Dyke Path round and under the canal to the road opposite. Turn right and cross the bridge over the Llangollen Canal and turn left immediately, still on the Acorn signed route. Keep the canal on your left to a bridge and turn left over it to the towpath on its lefthand side. Offa's Dyke Path goes off to your right at the bridge. For the remainder of the walk keep the canal on your right. In less than 2 miles pass Sun Trevor Inn on your right and 1/2 mile the path sign - Llangollen 1 1/2 miles - you still have 6 miles to go! Pass under bridge No. 43 and soon afterwards a swing bridge. 1/4 mile later you approach the moored boats and the Canal Wharf Museum. Llangollen lies below reached via steps but before descending continue ahead along the path - 2 miles to Horseshoe Falls. Pass bridges Nos 46 and 48 and the Llangollen

Motor Museum on your left. Here you walk across a small aqueduct and the canal channel swings left to the Chain Bridge Hotel and River Bar. Walk on the right of the hotel and keep ahead on the path to the semi-circular Horseshoe Falls; a beautiful idyllic spot. Retrace you steps back to the Canal Museum and descend to Llangollen crossing the bridge into the town - Market Street is a little way up on your right for the Bus Station. Here the walk ends - well done, you deserve my admiration - I hope you enjoyed it!

LLANGOLLEN - is world famous for the annual International Musical Eisteddfod held for six days in early July. The Llangollen Canal Wharf has a small museum and where you can take a horse drawn boat trip on the canal.

Trevor and the start of the section to Llangollen.

Horse Drawn Boat - Thomas Telford - near Llangollen Canal Wharf.

Horseshoe Falls.

PLACES TO STAY - A RANDOM SELECTION
- full lists from local Tourist Offices - see How To Do section.

Camping -

Nantwich - Brookfield Caravan Park, Shrewbridge Road. Tel. 01270 - 569176
Grindley Brook - beside staircase locks.
Ellesmere - Talbot Caravan Park, Talbot Street, Ellesmere. Tel. 01691 - 622285
Lyneal - Fernwood Caravan Park, Lyneal, Nr. Ellesmere. Tel. 01948 - 710221
Several around Llangollen.

Hotels & B.& B. -

Nantwich -
Lamb Hotel, Hospital Street, Nantwich. Tel. 01270 - 625286
The Malbank Hotel, 14, Beam Street, Nantwich. Tel 01270 - 626011
The Brambles - Mrs. Joy Jones, 2A Heathside, Nantwich. Tel. 01270 - 624664
The Limes - Mrs. J. Chesters, 5, Park Road, Nantwich. Tel. 01270 - 624081

Wrenbury -
Sproston Hill Cottage - Janet Wilkinson, Wrenbury. Tel 01270 - 780241. - 300 yards
from canal.

Ellesmere - contact Meres Visitor Centre. Tel. 01691 - 622981

Chirk -
Pedlar Corner, Colliery Road, Chirk. Tel. 01691 - 772903
The Lodge Country House,Parkgate, Halton, Chirk. Tel 01691 - 774424

Llangollen -
Hand Hotel, Bridge Street. Tel. 01978 - 860303
Cambrian House, Berwyn Street, Tel. 01978 - 861418
Adanhurst, Abbey Road, Tel. 01978 - 860562

Cefn y Fedw Farmhouse, Wrexham. LL14 1VA	Spacious stone farmhouse high above Garth & Trevor villages near Llangollen - an area of oustanding landscape - en suite, good food from £19.00 per person. Tel/Fax 01978 - 823403

**Mrs Joan Morris,
Gwernydd Farm, Garth,
Llangollen, Denbighshire.
LL20 7UR
Tel. 01978 - 820122**

Have a welcome break on a working dairy & sheep farm. Extensive views south. Tea/coffee making facilities, TV in bedrooms. Good food. Visitor's lounge. Horse riding by arrangement. Close to Offa's Dyke Path & Panorama walk. Llangollen 3 miles. Chester 20miles.W.T.B. Welcome Home - Highly Commended. Grid Ref. SJ264429.

The Waterways Code

1. Always be aware of other users.

2. Have extra regard for boaters mooring and anglers fishing.

3. Keep safety in mind when fishing, cycling and using locks.

4. Leave the canal as you wish to find it.

5. Follow organisers' requests at events.

6. Let others enjoy.

River Dee in Llangollen.

LOG

Date started and time ....

Date Completed and time ....

PLACE	MILE No.	COMMENTS
Nantwich	0	
Hurleston Jnc	2.5	
Wrenbury	9	
Grindley Brook	14.5	
Whitchurch	15.5	
Prees Branch	21.5	
Ellesmere	27.5	
Frankton Jnc	32.5	
Chirk Aueduct	38	
Chirk	38.5	
Pontcysyllte Aqueduct	42.5	
Trevor	43	
Llangollen	46.5	
Horseshoe Falls	48.5	
Llangollen	51	

THE LLANGOLLEN CANAL WALK BADGE

Complete the walk in this book and get the above special embroidered badge and signed certificate. Badges are blue cloth with lettering and aqueduct embroidered in four colours.

BADGE ORDER FORM

Date walks completed...

NAME ....

ADDRESS ....

....

Price: £5.00 each including postage, packing, VAT and signed completion certificate. Amount enclosed (Payable to The John Merrill Foundation) ..
From: The John Merrill Foundation,
32, Holmesdale,
Waltham Cross, Herts. EN8 8QY
Fax 01992 - 762776
********** YOU MAY PHOTOCOPY THIS FORM ***********

"HAPPY WALKING!" T SHIRT
- Yellow (daisy) with black lettering and walking man logo.
Send £8.95 to The John Merrill Foundation., stating size required.
Happy walking embroidered, full length zipped, Fleece Jacket - £17.95

EQUIPMENT NOTES
.....some personal thoughts from John N. Merru

Today there is a bewildering variety of walking gear, much is superfluous to general walking in Britain. As a basic observation, people over dress for the outdoors. Basically equipment should be serviceable and do the task. I don't approve of walking poles; humans were built to walk with two legs! The following are some of my throughts gathered from my walking experiences.

<u>BOOTS -</u> For summer use and day walking I wear lightweight boots. For high mountains and longer trips I prefer a good quality boot with a full leather upper, of medium weight, with a vibram sole. I always add a foam cushioned insole to help cushion the base of my feet.

<u>SOCKS -</u> I generally wear two thick pairs as this helps minimise blisters. The inner pair are of loop stitch variety and approximately 80% wool. The outer are a thick rib pair of approximately 80% wool.

<u>CLOTHES & WATERPROOFS -</u> for general walking I wear a T shirt or cotton shirt with a cotton wind jacket on top, and shorts - even in snow! You generate heat as you walk and I prefer to layer my clothes to avoid getting too hot. Depending on the season will dictate how many layers you wear. In soft rain I just use my wind jacket for I know it quickly dries out. In heavy or consistant rain I slip on a poncho, which covers my pack and allows air to circulate, while keeping dry. Only in extreme conditions will I don overtrousers, much preferring to get wet and feel comfortable. I never wear gaiters!

<u>FOOD -</u> as I walk I carry bars of chocolate, for they provide instant energy and are light to carry. In winter a flask of hot coffee is welcome. I never carry water and find no hardship from not doing so, but this is a personal matter! From experience I find the more I drink the more I want and sweat. You should always carry some extra food such as trail mix & candy bars etc., for emergencies.

<u>RUCKSACKS -</u> for day walking I use a climbing rucksack of about 40 litre capacity and although it leaves excess space it does mean that the sac is well padded, with an internal frame and padded shoulder straps. Inside apart from the basics for one day in winter I carry gloves, balaclava, spare pullover and a pair of socks.

<u>MAP & COMPASS</u> - when I am walking I always have the relevant map - preferably 1:25,000 scale - open in my hand. This enables me to constantly check that I am walking the right way. In case of bad weather I carry a compass, which once mastered gives you complete confidence in thick cloud or mist.

OBSERVE THE HIKER'S CODE

✻ Hike only along marked routes - do not leave the trail.

✻ Use stiles to climb fences; close gates.

✻ Camp only in designated campsites.

✻ Carry a light-weight stove.

✻ Leave the trail cleaner than you found it.

✻ Leave flowers and plants for others to enjoy.

✻ Keep dogs on a leash.

✻ Protect and do not disturb wildlife.

✻ Use the trail at your own risk.

✻ Leave only your thanks and footprints - take nothing but photographs.

Why I walk

I am often asked why I walk and to be truthful it is not easy to answer. I believe that walking gives you total freedom and at the same time getting some exercise without causing injuries like jogging. Freedom means the choice of walking at your own pace through a variety of countryside and looking and learning its secrets as you pass through. Freedom means the basics of life and you are master of your destiny.

When I set off for the day I carry all I need on my back, be it for a day walk or an extended walk over days or months. I leave behind the trappings of modern life and break many of the accepted rules of walking, by walking alone, not informing anyone of where I am going and what my expected return is. I feel such niceties are restrictive and hinder one's freedom to dwell on places or extend the walk. I admit one must be careful and if conditions detrioate one must descend or seek shelter. Walking alone and facing the problems on the way enable one to know oneself totally and know how one reacts to situations and one's limitations. I don't carry a mobile phone for this is a trapping of modern life. To be out walking in solitude and suddenly the phone rings is an alarming thought; how can one be at peace with the countryside?

I walk not just for health but to see and explore an area of countryside. To follow a path by a stream and see a kingfisher flash by, or watch a dipper bobbing up and down on a rock are one of the delights and enchanting moments on a walk. To walk in Spring and see the different flowers emerging, the birds gathering twigs for their nests, the trees in bud and new leaves unfolding bring added pleasure to the scene. To walk into a village and look at the houses as you past, see the date stone or see a cheese press or stocks help to bring the village alive and see its past history. To look at the hall or other principal building, the inn with an unusual name makes one want to know more and perhaps at a later date a visit to the local history department of the nearby library to discover more. The church - the open book of village life - always deserves exploration. To wander around the gravestones and see the dates and inscriptions. To walk inside and see the ancient font or old tomb gives greater understanding to the walk.

I walk in the minimum of clothes for freedom. Only in winter do I wear long trousers preferring to wear shorts and a T shirt most of the time. Even in rain I prefer walking in shorts with a poncho keeping dry but allowing maximum movement and freedom. Boots are worn whatever the walk but a lightweight pair for use in a dry summer and a more heavier and leather boot for winter or rain. A camera and binoculars to record and see distant mountains or birds; and for seeking out the blazed route ahead or for locating a stile.

Whilst there is the undeniable joy of exploring the area being walked through there is the added challenge of effort and fitness. I don't believe I walk fast just a steady 3 miles (5km) per hour, which I maintain without a rest during the day. I walk anything between 8 to 12 hours everyday, for days on end. I enjoy the mastery of walking up hill and dale and being able to push myself to walk further. Alternatively knowing I have thirty miles to walk, that day, and being able to pace oneself and complete the task still feeling fit and no pain. Knowing also that I can walk further if necessary. I don't train for a long walk simply preferring to set off and walk myself in as I progress.

Walking is spiritual. Yes, I believe in God and I have prayed often on a walk for help and guidance and have never been let down. I have also thanked him for the wonders I have seen on the way. Who cannot be moved when ascending to a pass and seeing sprawled out before you some incredibly beautiful scene. Who can wonder that after ten days alone in the wilderness that I reach the precise point I have been walking to. Yes, it is skill but I have been helped along the way and "shown" the route.

Walking is addictive but not compulsive. I find no hardship in walking day after day a marathon or more with forty pounds or more on my back. I never want to give up and can't wait to start again in the morning. The return from a long walk means a day walk has little meaning and for a while I peer out of the window but find it hard to put on the boots. But after a while as I have readjusted back a little I become restless and "angry" and put the boots on and walk for a few hours. If after that I have not been out for a few days I start to get withdrawal symptoms and have to break free and go for a walk.

So walking for me is a way of life, giving me the freedom to explore the countryside at my own pace. No other hobby or job gives you so much - exercise, experience. delight. discovery. adventure and exploration at such a minimal cost. It is man's simplest form of travel - on foot - and the only way to explore the world.

OTHER CANAL WALK GUIDES by John N. Merrill

VOL ONE - DERBYSHIRE AND NOTTINGHAMSHIRE - More than 25 walks, both short and long, on the Erewash, Derby, Trent & Mersey, Nottingham, Beeston and Nutbrook canals. The guide is not just a walk guide but a historical guide to what can be seen today and a photographic essay to canals in the area. 132 pages 60 photographs 32 maps ISBN 1-903627-53-2 £10.95

VOL TWO - CHESHIRE AND STAFFORDSHIRE - Details more than 40 circular walks on the Peak Forest, Macclesfield Caldon and Trent & Mersey canals. Like Vol. 1, a major reference source to canal walking on the western side of the Pennines. All are circular and include both long and short walks with numerous pubs along the way.
88 pages 61 photographs 27 maps ISBN 0 907496 38 5 Wire bound. £8.95

VOL THREE—STAFFORDSHIRE - 36 short circular walks on the Trent & Mersey, Coventry, Staffordshire & Worcestershire Canals within the boundary of Staffordshire, between Stoke on Trent and Burton Upon Trent. This book links together Vol. 1 & 2 of the series. 84 pages 60 photographs 30 maps ISBN 0 907496 62 8 Wire bound £8.95

VOL FOUR—THE CHESHIRE RING - Walk guide with history notes to the 97 mile walk around the ring on the Macclesfield, Peak Forest, Ashton, Rochdale, Bridgewater, and Trent & Mersey Canals. Comprehensive amenities guide to enable you to walk it in stages or as a weeks walk. 80 pages 38 photographs 15 maps ISBN 0 907496 63 6 £8.95

VOL SIX—SOUTH YORKSHIRE - Twenty-five walks on the Barnsley Canal, Dearne & Dove Canal, River Don and Navigation, Stainforth and Keadby Canal and Sheffield Canal. 84 pages 50 photographs 30 maps ISBN 0 907496 65 2 £6.95

WALKING THE DERBY CANAL RING - A magnificent 28 mile walk from the centre of Derby, following the line of the Derby Canal to the Trent & Mersey Canal and onto the River Trent and Erewash Canal. You return to Derby along the line of the Sandiacre section of the Derby Canal. ISBN 1874754 28 4. 32 pages. 5 maps. 10 photographs. £4.95

SHORT CIRCULAR WALKS ON THE CHESTERFIELD CANAL by John N. Merrill Twenty circular walks - 3 to 8 miles long, exploring the full length of the canal from Chesterfield to West Stockwith and the River Trent. Including walking the Cuckoo Way, the canal end to end - 42 miles. ISBN 1-903627-43-5 128 pages. 22 maps. 60 photographs. £9.95

VOL SEVEN—THE TRENT & MERSEY CANAL by John N. Merrill - Walk guide to the whole length of the canal—end-to-end—from Runcorn to Preston Brook and onto Shardlow and Derwent Mouth. 100 miles of some of the finest canal walking in Britain. Amenities guide and walk described in stages. 68 pages 35 photographs 12 maps ISBN 1 874754 19 5.   £6.95

VOL. EIGHT - WALKING THE LLANGOLLEN CANAL by John N. Merrill. A complete end to end walk from Nantwich to Llangollen -51 miles, along the canl. The scenery is oustanding and the canal features are unsurpassed. ISBN 1 84173-017-3 56 pages. 22 photographs. 10 maps. £6.95

SHORT CIRCULAR WALKS ON THE CROMFORD CANAL by John N. Merrill. Eleven walks covering the whole canal from Cromford to Langley Mill.
84 pages, wire bound, 12 maps. 40 photographs.
ISBN 1-903627-54-0 £8.95

SHORT CIRCULAR WALKS ON THE GRANTHAM CANAL by John N. Merrill - Fifteen walks on the Grantham Canal. 100 pages 60 photographs 16 maps ISBN 1 903627 56 7. £9.95

SHORT CIRCULAR WALKS ON THE RIVER LEE NAVIGATION by John N. Merrill - 10 circular walks - 5 to 6 miles long - on the navigation between Ponders End and Hertford; all interlink. Magnificent walking in the Lee Valley, just north of London. 60 pages, 10 maps, 20 photograpghs. ISBN 1-903627-68-0 £5.95

Nantwich Canal Centre.

OTHER JOHN MERRILL WALK BOOKS

CIRCULAR WALK GUIDES -
SHORT CIRCULAR WALKS IN THE PEAK DISTRICT - Vol. 1,2, 3 and 9
CIRCULAR WALKS IN WESTERN PEAKLAND
SHORT CIRCULAR WALKS IN THE STAFFORDSHIRE MOORLANDS
SHORT CIRCULAR WALKS - TOWNS & VILLAGES OF THE PEAK DISTRICT
SHORT CIRCULAR WALKS AROUND MATLOCK
SHORT CIRCULAR WALKS IN "PEAK PRACTICE COUNTRY."
SHORT CIRCULAR WALKS IN THE DUKERIES
SHORT CIRCULAR WALKS IN SOUTH YORKSHIRE
SHORT CIRCULAR WALKS IN SOUTH DERBYSHIRE
SHORT CIRCULAR WALKS AROUND BUXTON
SHORT CIRCULAR WALKS AROUND WIRKSWORTH
SHORT CIRCULAR WALKS IN THE HOPE VALLEY
40 SHORT CIRCULAR WALKS IN THE PEAK DISTRICT
CIRCULAR WALKS ON KINDER & BLEAKLOW
SHORT CIRCULAR WALKS IN SOUTH NOTTINGHAMSHIRE
SHORT CIRCULAR WALKS IN CHESHIRE
SHORT CIRCULAR WALKS IN WEST YORKSHIRE
WHITE PEAK DISTRICT AIRCRAFT WRECKS
CIRCULAR WALKS IN THE DERBYSHIRE DALES
SHORT CIRCULAR WALKS FROM BAKEWELL
SHORT CIRCULAR WALKS IN LATHKILL DALE
CIRCULAR WALKS IN THE WHITE PEAK
SHORT CIRCULAR WALKS IN EAST DEVON
SHORT CIRCULAR WALKS AROUND HARROGATE
SHORT CIRCULAR WALKS IN CHARNWOOD FOREST
SHORT CIRCULAR WALKS AROUND CHESTERFIELD
SHORT CIRCULAR WALKS IN THE YORKS DALES - Vol 1 - Southern area.
SHORT CIRCULAR WALKS IN THE AMBER VALLEY (Derbyshire)
SHORT CIRCULAR WALKS IN THE LAKE DISTRICT
SHORT CIRCULAR WALKS IN THE NORTH YORKSHIRE MOORS
SHORT CIRCULAR WALKS IN EAST STAFFORDSHIRE
DRIVING TO WALK - 16 Short Circular walks south of London by Dr. Simon Archer Vol 1 and 2
LONG CIRCULAR WALKS IN THE PEAK DISTRICT - Vol.1, 2 , 3, 4 and 5.
DARK PEAK AIRCRAFT WRECK WALKS
LONG CIRCULAR WALKS IN THE STAFFORDSHIRE MOORLANDS
LONG CIRCULAR WALKS IN CHESHIRE
WALKING THE TISSINGTON TRAIL
WALKING THE HIGH PEAK TRAIL
WALKING THE MONSAL TRAIL & SETT VALLEY TRAILS
PEAK DISTRICT WALKING - TEN "TEN MILER'S" - Vol One and Two
CLIMB THE PEAKS OF THE PEAK DISTRICT
PEAK DISTRICT WALK A MONTH Vols One,Two, Three, Four, Five & Six
TRAIN TO WALK Vol. One - The Hope Valley Line
DERBYSHIRE LOST VILLAGE WALKS -Vol One and Two.
CIRCULAR WALKS IN DOVEDALE AND THE MANIFOLD VALLEY
CIRCULAR WALKS AROUND GLOSSOP
WALKING THE LONGDENDALE TRAIL
WALKING THE UPPER DON TRAIL
SHORT CIRCULAR WALKS IN CANNOCK CHASE
CIRCULAR WALKS IN THE DERWENT VALLEY
WALKING THE TRAILS OF NORTH-EAST DERBYSHIRE
WALKING THE PENNINE BRIDLEWAY & CIRCULAR WALKS
SHORT CIRCULAR WALKS ON THE RIVER LEE NAVIGATION
SHORT CIRCULAR WALKS ON THE NEW RIVER & SOUTH-EAST HERTFORDSHIRE
SHORT CIRCULAR WALKS IN EPPING FOREST

CANAL WALKS -
VOL 1 - DERBYSHIRE & NOTTINGHAMSHIRE
VOL 2 - CHESHIRE & STAFFORDSHIRE
VOL 3 - STAFFORDSHIRE
VOL 4 - THE CHESHIRE RING
VOL 5 - THE GRANTHAM CANAL
VOL 6 - SOUTH YORKSHIRE
VOL 7 - THE TRENT & MERSEY CANAL
VOL 8 - WALKING THE DERBY CANAL RING
VOL 9 - WALKING THE LLANGOLLEN CANAL
VOL 10 - CIRCULAR WALKS ON THE CHESTERFIELD CANAL
VOL 11 - CIRCULAR WALKS ON THE CROMFORD CANAL
Vol.13 - SHORT CICULAR WALKS ON THE RIVER LEE NAVIGATION

JOHN MERRILL DAY CHALLENGE WALKS -
WHITE PEAK CHALLENGE WALK
THE HAPPY HIKER - WHITE PEAK - CHALLENGE WALK No.2
DARK PEAK CHALLENGE WALK
PEAK DISTRICT END TO END WALKS
STAFFORDSHIRE MOORLANDS CHALLENGE WALK
THE LITTLE JOHN CHALLENGE WALK
YORKSHIRE DALES CHALLENGE WALK

For a free complete catalogue of John Merrill walk Guides write to The John Merrill Foundation